Very
MAPLE SYRUP

Very MAPLE SYRUP

JENNIFER TRAINER THOMPSON

Celestial Arts
Berkeley | Toronto

Celestial Arts
P. O. Box 7123
Berkeley, California 94707
www.tenspeed.com

Distributed in Australia by Simon and Schuster Australia, in Canada by
Ten Speed Press Canada, in New Zealand by Southern Publishers Group,
in South Africa by Real Books, and in the United Kingdom and Europe by
Airlift Book Company.

Cover and text design by Susanne Weihl

Library of Congress Cataloging-in-Publication Data
Thompson, Jennifer Trainer.
  Very maple syrup / Jennifer Trainer Thompson.
    p. cm.
  ISBN 1-58761-181-3
  1. Cookery (Maple sugar and syrup) 2. Maple syrup. I. Title.
TX767.M3.T48 2003
  641.6′364—dc21   2003013314

Printed in Singapore
First printing, 2003

1 2 3 4 5 6 7 8 9 10—07 06 05 04 03

Acknowledgments

I'd like to thank Lynn Danahy, Jim Starke,
Jody Fijal, Cathy Greenwald, Jeannie and David Aplin,
and especially Linda Stripp for their assistance with this book.

Contents

The gift of the sugar maple trees is from a benevolent Providence.

—Benjamin Rush (a signer of
the Declaration of Independence),
in a letter to Thomas Jefferson

Introduction

It's early March in New England, and while the nights are still cold and frosty, the days are warm enough that you can feel the sun's feeble heat. That "give and take" of cold nights and warm days creates a suction of sorts in maple trees that causes the sap to rise and flow and yield its sweet water. There aren't any buds on the trees yet, but Yankees know the first sign of spring: galvanized buckets hanging from maple trees along the side of the road.

When I was a kid, we cooked down our own maple syrup in the woods behind the Orchard School (forty gallons of sap to make one gallon of syrup), and that event became a cherished childhood school memory. More recently, when I enrolled our son in nursery school in the Berkshire Hills of northwestern Massachusetts, it wasn't the terrific program, or the brightly colored classroom, or even the wonderful teachers that sold me: it was the fact that the kids went into the woods, tapped the trees, and made their own maple syrup. My son came home from school thrilled the day he got to taste the sap dripping from the spigot; he was startled by how clear it was (like water), and how mild the sweetness. Pancakes have been a Saturday-morning ritual ever since.

While sweeteners have been around for at least three thousand years, it was the Native Americans who discovered that sugar could be tapped from trees. Long before Europeans arrived in North America, Native Americans were collecting "tree water" from maple trees and cooking it down over an open fire. Once they boiled the excess water from the sap, the remaining maple sugar was stored in cakes for the entire year. The Algonquin name for maple sugar is *Sinsibuckwud* ("drawn from the wood"), while the Ojibway called it *sheesheegummavvis* ("sap flows fast").

The Native Americans taught the Pilgrims and early settlers throughout New England and Canada how to tap trees and make maple syrup. Indeed, maple syrup was part of the menu at the 1621 Thanksgiving in Plymouth. The Iroquois even celebrated the spring with "maple moon" or "sugar month" religious festivals that involved a maple dance performed when trees were tapped.

Maple sugar and maple syrup were supplemented by sugar refined from sugarcane during the 1600s, and sugar production was the biggest and most lucrative industry in the Caribbean and Central America. By the late 1600s, Europeans and people in the new colonies were drinking coffee and tea regularly, which led to increased demand for sugar. Throughout the 1600s, tremendous numbers of Africans were enslaved and brought to the Caribbean islands to work the sugar, tobacco, and cotton plantations, and the "sugar islands" of the Caribbean brought vast wealth to the French and English. As the slave trade grew, so did the antislavery movement. Interestingly, the movement to abolish the slave trade led to increased maple syrup production, which was an alternative to refined sugar. The March *Farmer's Almanack* of 1803, for example, admonished farmers to "prepare for making maple sugar, which is more pleasant and patriotic than that ground by the hand of slavery, and boiled down by the heat of misery." During the Civil War, maple syrup production became a matter of patriotism; not only did soldiers need food that wouldn't spoil during shipment and storage, but the use of maple sugar to sweeten one's foods was regarded as an act of protest by Northerners, since all the cane sugar and most of the molasses was produced in the South.

Today, most maple syrup—still a spring tradition steeped in ritual and romance—is produced in Vermont, New York, Ohio, Michigan, Pennsylvania, New Hampshire, and Canada. You won't find maple sugaring below 35 degrees latitude or west of 95 degrees longitude. Weather is the most significant role in sap production, with farmers relying on freezing nights and thaws during the day, which occurs anywhere from late February to early April. The sugar content of the sap is higher in a sugar maple than any other type of maple, and better tasting, according to many.

The federal government grades the syrup by color and flavor: grade A light amber, grade A medium amber, grade A dark amber, and grade B. Which is best is a matter of taste. In general, the lighter the color, the more delicate the flavor. "First-run sap," which is produced early in the season, tends to yield a light, delicate syrup. "The first run," wrote naturalist John Burroughs, "like first love, is always the best, always the fullest, always the sweetest; while there is a purity and delicacy of flavor about the sugar that far surpasses any subsequent yield."

If you'd like to try your hand at maple sugaring, the following sources can help: *Making Maple Syrup* by Noel Perrin, *The Maple Sugar Book* by Helen and Scott Nearing, the website of the Cornell Sugar Maple Research and Extension Program (http://maple.dnr.cornell .edu/produc/FAQIndex.asp), and the North American Maple Syrup Producers Manual (ohioline.ag.ohio-state.edu). If you just want to enjoy the flavor, the following recipes offer a variety of ways to use pure maple syrup.

The maple-tree yields a Sap,

which has a much pleasanter taste than the best Limonade or Cherry-water,

and makes the wholesomest drink in the World.

—Louis, Baron de La Hontan, 1703

Salads and Starters

Roasted Butternut Squash Bisque with Maple Crème Fraîche

Adding a teaspoon of curry powder to the onions while they are sautéing gives this warming winter soup an interesting twist.

- $^1_2$ cup crème fraîche
- 1 tablespoon maple syrup
- 1 $^1_4$ teaspoons kosher salt
- 2 tablespoons unsalted butter
- 1 cup finely chopped yellow onions
- 1 clove garlic, minced
- 1 butternut squash, peeled, seeded, and cut into 1-inch cubes (about 6 cups)
- 2 tablespoons canola oil
- 3 $^1_2$ cups vegetable stock or chicken stock
- 1 cup heavy cream

Preheat the oven to 425 F. In a small bowl, mix the crème fraîche, maple syrup, and $^1_4$ teaspoon of the salt together until blended.

In large soup pot, melt the butter over medium heat. Add the onion and garlic. Sauté for 5 minutes, or until golden. Set aside.

In a bowl, combine the butternut squash, oil, and the remaining 1 teaspoon salt. Toss to coat evenly. Spread on a baking sheet and roast for 20 minutes, or until easily pierced with a fork. Remove from the oven and add to the soup pot. Add the vegetable stock and cook over medium heat for 20 minutes or until tender. Remove from the heat and let cool slightly. Add the heavy cream. Purée in a blender in several batches. Return to the pot and gently reheat. Ladle into bowls. Top each serving with 1 tablespoon maple crème fraîche and serve hot.

Serves 4 to 6

Maple Cornmeal Oysters with Spicy Mayo

Unshucked raw oysters can be kept in the refrigerator for 3 to 5 days. Make sure the shells are closed tightly; cover them loosely with a damp cloth and keep in an airy place. Oysters are best paired with a Riesling, Sauvignon Blanc, or Chardonnay.

$\frac{1}{4}$ cup mayonnaise, preferably homemade

$\frac{1}{2}$ teaspoon minced chipotle chile in adobe sauce, minced

$\frac{1}{4}$ cup canola oil

$\frac{1}{2}$ cup cornmeal

$\frac{1}{2}$ teaspoon kosher salt

$\frac{1}{4}$ teaspoon cayenne pepper

12 raw oysters, shucked and shredded

$\frac{1}{4}$ cup maple syrup

In a small bowl, combine the mayonnaise and chipotle. Mix well and set aside.

In a small bowl, combine the cornmeal, salt, and cayenne pepper. Stir to blend. Drain and pat the oysters dry with paper towels. Dip the oysters in the maple syrup and then in the cornmeal mixture. Coat well.

In a small skillet, heat the oil over medium-high heat. Fry the oysters for 30 seconds to 1 minute on each side, or until golden. Drain on paper towels. Serve at once with the chipotle mayonnaise.

Serves 2

Baked Brie with Maple Syrup Glaze

Be sure to buy a Brie wheel rather than a slice from a wheel. It's worth spending a few extra dollars for a good-quality Brie from a cheese shop.

3 $1\frac{1}{2}$ tablespoons maple syrup
2 tablespoons unsalted butter, melted
$\frac{1}{4}$ cup sliced almonds, toasted
1 round Brie (about 8 ounces)
2 tablespoons unsalted butter
1 Granny Smith apple, peeled, cored, and thinly sliced
Crackers, for serving

Preheat the oven to 350 F. Spray a baking sheet with vegetable-oil cooking spray.

In a small bowl, mix $1\frac{1}{2}$ tablespoons of the maple syrup and the melted butter together until well blended. Stir in the almonds. Place the Brie on the prepared pan and spoon the almond maple mixture over the top. Bake for 15 minutes, or until gooey.

In a small skillet, melt the butter over medium heat and add the remaining 2 tablespoons syrup. Add the apple slices and sauté for 5 minutes, or until softened. Remove from the heat and overlap the apple slices in a circle in the center of a plate. Remove the Brie from the oven and place it in the center of the apples. Serve immediately, with crackers.

Serves 8

Autumn Salad with Maple-Thyme Vinaigrette

Stilton cheese has more moisture than other types of blue cheese. The moisture content makes it more difficult to crumble, but its significantly sharper flavor is worth the effort.

Maple-Thyme Vinaigrette

- 1 tablespoon minced shallot
- 2 tablespoons cider vinegar
- $\frac{1}{4}$ teaspoon Dijon mustard
- $\frac{1}{2}$ teaspoon kosher salt
- 2 tablespoons maple syrup
- 2 tablespoons chopped fresh thyme
- $\frac{1}{2}$ cup walnut oil

- 2 unpeeled red Gala or Granny Smith apples, cored and thinly sliced
- 2 tablespoons freshly squeezed lemon juice
- 8 cups baby salad greens
- 1 cup sliced red onion
- 1 cup crumbled Stilton cheese
- 1 teaspoon kosher salt

To make the vinaigrette, combine all the ingredients in a small bowl and whisk until blended. Set aside.

Put the apples in a large bowl. Toss with lemon juice. Add the greens, red onion, cheese, and salt. Toss to combine. Add the dressing and toss to coat. Divide among 4 plates and serve immediately.

Serves 4

Winter Salad with Roasted Shallot-Maple Vinaigrette

This versatile dressing is delicious on many salads, but especially appreciated in the winter, when we're looking for variety in our greens.

Roasted Shallot-Maple Vinaigrette

> 2 tablespoons olive oil
> 1 small shallot
> 1 clove garlic
> $1/2$ teaspoon Dijon mustard
> $1 1/2$ tablespoons maple syrup
> 2 tablespoons sherry or balsamic vinegar
> 1 teaspoon salt
> Freshly ground black pepper
>
> 6 cups loosely packed baby salad greens
> $1/4$ cup coarsely chopped roasted pistachios
> 2 ounces goat cheese, crumbled

To make the vinaigrette, preheat the oven to 400 F. In a small baking dish, combine the olive oil, shallot, and garlic. Cover with aluminum foil and roast for 15 minutes, or until easily pierced with a fork. Strain the olive oil and set aside, reserving the shallot and garlic. Let cool.

In a blender or food processor, combine the reserved shallot, garlic, mustard, maple syrup, vinegar, and salt. Blend until smooth. With the machine running, gradually add the reserved olive oil in thin stream. Season with pepper.

In a large bowl, combine the greens and pistachios. Toss with a little of the vinaigrette until lightly coated. Taste and adjust seasoning. Divide the tossed greens among 4 plates and top with the goat cheese.

Serves 4

Maple-Garlic Chipotle Wings

Chipotles, which are smoked jalapeño chiles, lend a subtle smokiness to many dishes.

Sauce

> 3 chipotle chiles (seeded if you prefer less heat)
>
> $1/2$ cup canola oil
>
> 3 cloves garlic
>
> $1/4$ cup maple syrup
>
> 1 teaspoon freshly ground black pepper
>
> $2 1/2$ pounds chicken wings
>
> Pickled jalapeño chile rings, for garnish

Preheat the oven to 425 F. Line a baking sheet with parchment paper.

To make the sauce, purée the chipotles in a blender. Add the remaining sauce ingredients, and blend until smooth.

Arrange the wings on the prepared pan and sprinkle with pepper on both sides. Bake for 15 minutes. Remove from the oven and turn the wings over. Preheat the broiler. Brush the wings with the sauce and broil for 3 minutes. Remove and turn, baste with the sauce and broil for 2 minutes on the second side, or until crispy. Remove, brush with any remaining sauce, and arrange on a serving plate. Sprinkle liberally with pickled jalapeño rings and serve.

Serves 6

I have never tasted any better sugar
than what has been made from the maple, when it has been properly refined.
It has a peculiarly rich, salubrious, and pleasant taste.

—Samuel Williams, *A Natural and Civil History of Vermont*, 1794

Side Dishes

Maple Roasted Root Vegetables

To ensure even cooking, cut all the vegetables to the same size.

> 2 beets, peeled and cut into 1-inch cubes
> 1 celery root or turnip, peeled and cut into 1-inch cube
> 1 carrot, peeled and cut into 1-inch rounds
> 1 sweet potato, peeled and cut into 1-inch rounds
> 2 parsnips, peeled and cut into 1-inch rounds
> $\frac{1}{2}$ yellow onion, cut into 1-inch cubes
> 3 tablespoons plus 1 teaspoon canola oil
> 1 teaspoon salt
> 1 tablespoon minced fresh rosemary
> 2 tablespoons maple syrup

Preheat the oven to 425 F. Cook the beets in boiling salted water for 3 minutes. Using a slotted spoon, transfer to a bowl of ice water to cool. Drain and set aside. Put all the remaining vegetables in a medium bowl and toss with the 3 tablespoons oil. Add the salt and rosemary. In a separate bowl, toss the beets in the 1 teaspoon oil. Spread all the vegetables on a baking sheet in one layer. Roast, tossing occasionally, for 20 minutes, or until soft when pressed. Remove from the oven, drizzle with the maple syrup and gently toss to coat. Return to oven for 5 minutes, or until glazed. Serve hot.

Serves 6 to 8

Warm New Potatoes with Maple-Bacon Dressing

If you can't find new potatoes, small yukon gold potatoes are a good substitute. Serve this with grilled or roast fish.

  2 tablespoons olive oil

  3 slices bacon, chopped

  2 tablespoons minced shallots

  $\frac{1}{2}$ teaspoon minced garlic

  1 tablespoon toasted mustard seeds

  1 tablespoon maple syrup

  2 tablespoons cider vinegar

  1 teaspoon kosher salt

  2 tablespoons canola oil

  12 small new potatoes, washed and cut into quarters

In a small skillet, heat the olive oil over medium heat. Add the bacon and cook for 10 minutes, or until crispy. Add the shallots and garlic and sauté for 3 minutes, or until the shallots are translucent. Remove from the heat and stir in the mustard seeds, maple syrup, vinegar, and salt.

Cook the potatoes in salted boiling water for 10 minutes, or until tender. Drain and toss with the dressing.

Serves 4

Maple Baked Beans

Native Americas in what became New England flavored their baked beans with maple syrup. The Pilgrims learned how to make baked beans from Native Americans, but substituted molasses for the maple syrup.

1 tablespoon canola oil

$\frac{1}{2}$ cup chopped bacon

1 cup finely chopped onion

$\frac{1}{2}$ teaspoon salt

$\frac{1}{4}$ teaspoon freshly ground black pepper

1 teaspoon minced garlic

1 cup dried navy beans, soaked overnight

2 tablespoons firmly packed brown sugar

$\frac{1}{2}$ cup maple syrup

1 cup ketchup

$\frac{1}{2}$ teaspoon dry mustard

3 $\frac{1}{2}$ cups water

In a large pot, heat the oil over medium heat. Add the bacon and cook for 5 minutes, or until crisp. Add the onion and sauté for 3 minutes. Add the salt and pepper. Stir in the garlic and sauté for 1 minute, or until fragrant. Stir in all the remaining ingredients, mixing thoroughly. Bring to a simmer over medium-high heat and cook for 45 minutes, or until tender.

Preheat the oven to 300 F. Transfer the beans to a casserole dish, cover, and bake for 4 $\frac{1}{2}$ hours, or until tender, checking every hour and adding water as liquid is absorbed.

Serves 12

Smokey Maple-Black Bean Hash

Don't be daunted by the amount of salt in this recipe; the potatoes will absorb the salt and balance the flavors. Serve this hash with eggs for breakfast. Or, try spooning it into a flour tortilla with scrambled eggs and salsa.

2 tablespoons canola oil
1 cup chopped yellow onion
$\frac{1}{2}$ teaspoon minced garlic
$\frac{1}{2}$ cup coarsely chopped poblano pepper
1 cup coarsely chopped portobello mushroom cap
1 teaspoon salt
1 cup finely diced yukon gold potatoes
1 (15-ounce) can black beans, rinsed and drained
1 chipotle chile in adobo sauce, minced
$\frac{1}{4}$ cup vegetable stock or water
2 tablespoons maple syrup

Heat the oil in a large skillet over medium heat. Add the onions and sauté for 5 minutes, or until golden. Add the garlic, poblano, mushrooms, and salt and sauté for 5 more minutes, or until the garlic is lightly browned and the chiles are soft. Add all the remaining ingredients. Cover and simmer over medium-high heat for 10 minutes. Uncover and cook an additional 10 minutes, or until the liquid has evaporated.

Serves 5

Maple-Ginger Glazed Carrots

This side dish is simple and fast to prepare. Be careful not to overcook the carrots or they will turn mushy.

2 pounds carrots, peeled and cut into $1/4$-inch-thick rounds

$1/2$ cup water

1 teaspoon salt

5 tablespoons unsalted butter

2 tablespoons minced fresh ginger

$1/2$ cup maple syrup

2 tablespoons firmly packed brown sugar

In a large skillet, combine the carrots, water, salt, and 3 tablespoons of the butter. Bring to a simmer over medium heat, cover, and cook for 8 minutes, or until carrots just begin to soften. Uncover and add remaining 2 tablespoons butter, the ginger, maple syrup, and brown sugar. Continue cooking until all the liquid is absorbed. Serve hot.

Serves 6 to 8

Maple-Pecan Corn Bread Stuffing

This stuffing is also great for Cornish hens and as a bed for pork chops or roast chicken.

Corn Bread

    1 cup cornmeal

    $3/4$ cup all-purpose flour

    3 tablespoons sugar

    2 teaspoons baking powder

    $3/4$ teaspoon salt

    1 $1/4$ cups milk

    2 large eggs

    3 tablespoons unsalted butter, melted

    $1/4$ cup maple syrup

    1 cup pecans, toasted and chopped

    1 tablespoon unsalted butter

    1 cup finely chopped yellow onion

    1 stalk celery

    1 teaspoon minced garlic

    1 tablespoon minced fresh flat-leaf parsley

    $1/3$ cup chicken or vegetable stock

Preheat the oven to 375 F. Butter an 8-inch square baking dish.

To make the corn bread, combine the cornmeal, flour, sugar, baking powder, and salt in a medium bowl. Stir to blend well.

In a separate bowl, combine the milk, eggs, and butter. Whisk to blend. Add to the dry ingredients and stir to just combine. Pour the batter into the prepared dish and bake for 25 minutes, or until a toothpick inserted in the center comes out clean. Remove from the oven and let cool. Cut cornbread into $\frac{1}{2}$-inch dice; it may crumble when cut (you should have about 6 cups). Set aside.

In a small bowl, combine the syrup and pecans and mix well. In a large skillet, melt the butter over medium heat. Add the onion, celery, and garlic. Sauté for 5 minutes, or until the onion is golden. Add the parsley and sauté for 1 minute. Add the syrup mixture and corn bread and blend well. Add the stock and cook, stirring, until heated through.

Transfer the stuffing to an ovenproof serving dish and bake, covered, at 350 F for 15 minutes, or until lightly browned on top.

Makes 6 $\frac{1}{2}$ cups

Maple-Sweet Potato Casserole

This recipe is from my friend Jim Starke. If you want this dish sweet and retro, cover the top with mini marshmallows.

> 6 pounds sweet potatoes
> $\frac{1}{2}$ cup maple syrup
> $\frac{1}{4}$ cup unsalted butter
> Salt and freshly ground black pepper
> 1 (15-ounce) can whole cranberry sauce
> 1 cup mini marshmallows (optional)

Preheat the oven to 375 F. Butter a 9 by 12-inch baking dish.

Bake the sweet potatoes for $1\frac{1}{2}$ hours, or until fork tender. Let cool to room temperature. Scoop out the flesh and mash in a bowl. Add $\frac{1}{4}$ cup of the maple syrup, the butter, salt, and pepper to the mixture and whip. Spread half of the sweet potato in an even layer in the prepared dish. Spread the whole cranberry sauce over the sweet potatoes. Spread the second half of the sweet potatoes over the sauce. Spread the remaining $\frac{1}{4}$ cup maple syrup over the sweet potatoes. (If you like, cover evenly with marshmallows.) Cover with aluminum foil and bake for about 30 minutes, or until heated through. Uncover and bake for an additional 5 minutes to caramelize the maple syrup and brown the marshmallows, if using. Serve hot.

Serves 10

When made in small quantities . . . [maple syrup]
has a wild delicacy of flavor that no other sweet can match. What you
smell in freshly cut maple-wood, or taste in the blossom of the tree, is in it.
It is then indeed, the distilled essence of the tree.

—Naturalist John Burroughs, 1886

Main Courses

Maple Pulled Barbecued Pork

Pulled pork is delicious served as a hearty sandwich on a fresh baked roll (and better yet with coleslaw). The sauce will keep refrigerated for 2 weeks and frozen for up to 3 months; double the recipe for the sauce and keep it to use on grilled chicken and other meats.

1 tablespoon canola oil

1 cup chopped onion

1 teaspoon minced garlic

1 tablespoon ground cumin

1 tablespoon chile powder

1 teaspoon salt

$1/4$ teaspoon cayenne pepper

1 tablespoon yellow mustard

$1/4$ cup freshly squeezed orange juice

1 cup ketchup

1 tablespoon molasses

$1/4$ cup cider vinegar

$1/2$ cup maple syrup

$1/4$ cup water

$2 1/2$ pounds boneless pork loin, cut into 4 pieces

Kosher salt and freshly ground black pepper

In a medium saucepan, heat the oil over medium heat. Add the onion and sauté for 5 minutes, or until golden. Add the garlic and sauté for 1 minute, or until fragrant. Add all the remaining ingredients, except the pork, and simmer 30 minutes.

Adjust an oven rack in the middle of the oven. Preheat the oven to 275 F.

Season the pork with salt and freshly ground black pepper. Place in a roasting pan or casserole dish. Pour the sauce over the top, cover with aluminum foil, and bake, turning every hour, for 3 hours, or until fork tender. Remove from the oven and let cool. Pull or shred the meat apart with a fork. Stir the meat into the sauce and reheat.

Serves 8

Maple Glazed Ham

This will feed a crowd and is perfect for a buffet. (Even if you're not serving a crowd, leftovers will be welcome.) The cooking time remains the same for a boneless ham.

6- to 8-pound fully cooked, bone-in smoked ham

2 cups apple cider

2 cups water

1_4 cup firmly packed brown sugar

1_2 cup maple syrup

2 tablespoons prepared horseradish

1 tablespoon Dijon mustard

Preheat the oven to 325 F. Place the ham, fat side up, in a roasting pan. Pour the apple cider and water into the bottom of the pan. Bake the ham for 1 1_4 hours, or until completely heated through.

In a small bowl, combine the sugar, syrup, horseradish, and mustard. Stir to blend. Remove the ham from the oven and spread the maple mixture over the ham. Bake, basting the ham with the pan liquid every 15 minutes, for 45 minutes, or until the ham has darkened and the edges of the meat are crispy. Remove from the oven, carve, and serve warm.

Serves 8

Maple-Soy Marinated Skirt Steak

Skirt steak is a slightly tough cut of meat but extremely flavorful.

$3/4$ cup tamari
$1/2$ cup maple syrup
2 tablespoons canola oil
1 teaspoon minced garlic
1 teaspoon minced fresh ginger
2 tablespoons minced shallots
2 tablespoons sesame seeds
$1 1/2$ pounds skirt steak, cut into 4 pieces

In a glass or ceramic baking dish just large enough to hold the steak, combine all the ingredients except the steak. Stir to blend and add the steak. Let stand at room temperature for at least 30 minutes or up to 2 hours, turning several times.

Prepare a hot fire in a charcoal grill or heat an oiled grill pan over high heat. Remove the meat from the marinade and grill on each side for 3 minutes for medium-rare. Remove from the grill and let rest for 5 minutes. Cut, against the grain, into diagonal slices.

Serves 4

Grilled Lamb Chops with Mustard-Maple Glaze

This recipe is fast and easy to prepare. Save any extra glaze to brush on the chops before serving.

1 tablespoon canola oil
$1/4$ cup finely chopped onion
$1/2$ teaspoon minced garlic
$1/4$ cup Dijon mustard
$1/2$ cup maple syrup
1 teaspoon salt, plus additional for seasoning
$1/4$ teaspoon freshly ground black pepper, plus additional
    for seasoning
1 tablespoon unsalted butter
1 tablespoon minced fresh mint
8 baby lamb chops
Olive oil, for brushing

Heat the canola oil in medium skillet over medium heat. Add the onion and sauté for 3 minutes, or until translucent. Add the garlic and cook for 2 more minutes. Add the mustard and syrup and stir to combine. Cook for 5 minutes. Add the 1 teaspoon salt, the $1/4$ teaspoon pepper, butter, and mint. Stir to combine. Remove from the heat and set aside.

Prepare a hot fire in a charcoal grill or heat a grill pan over high heat. Brush both sides of each lamb chop with olive oil. Season with salt and pepper. Grill for 5 minutes on each side. Brush both sides of the chops with a generous amount of glaze and cook 1 more minute on each side for medium-rare.

Serves 4

Grilled Chicken with Maple-Rum Barbecue Sauce

With one foot in the islands and the other in New England, I love these two ingredients (maple syrup and rum), which team up so well here to combine heat and sweetness.

2 dried chipotle chiles, chopped

$1/4$ cup dark rum

$1/4$ cup maple syrup

$1/2$ cup ketchup

$1/2$ teaspoon dried oregano

$1/2$ teaspoon ground cinnamon

$1/2$ teaspoon ground allspice

6 boneless chicken breast halves

In a blender, blend the chipotles until ground. Add all the remaining ingredients except the chicken. Blend again until smooth. Pour into a glass or ceramic baking dish just large enough to hold the chicken and let stand for 1 hour. Add the breasts, turn to coat, and let stand for 1 hour.

Prepare a medium-hot fire in a charcoal grill or preheat a gas grill to medium. Grill for 5 to 7 minutes. Brush with sauce and turn. Grill for 5 to 7 minutes on the second side, or until opaque throughout. Transfer to plates and brush with additional sauce. Serve hot.

Serves 6

Maple-Rosemary Lamb Chops with Goat Cheese Stuffing

The headiness of the cheese and piney flavor of the rosemary blend beautifully with maple syrup.

4 lamb loin chops, each 1 inch thick
$\frac{1}{4}$ cup soft bread crumbs from day-old bread
1 $\frac{1}{2}$ teaspoons dried rosemary, crushed
$\frac{1}{2}$ teaspoon freshly ground black pepper
$\frac{1}{4}$ teaspoon freshly grated nutmeg
1 egg
1 tablespoon water
3 cloves garlic, minced
2 tablespoons goat cheese, at room temperature
1 $\frac{1}{2}$ tablespoons maple syrup

Slit the lamb chops horizontally to the bone, splitting them but not separating them. In a small bowl, combine the bread crumbs, rosemary, pepper, and nutmeg. Add the egg, water, garlic, and goat cheese. Let set until the mixture firms up, about 20 minutes. Stuff the lamb chops and close the open side of each with a few toothpicks. Brush lightly with a little maple syrup to glaze.

Preheat the broiler. Place the chops on a broiler pan and broil for 1 $\frac{1}{2}$ minutes on each side for rare, or 2 minutes for medium-rare.

Serves 2

Grilled Pork Chops with Maple-Garlic Grill Sauce

Driven by the garlic, this sauce makes a great marinade and grill sauce.

6 cloves garlic
Juice of 1 lemon
1 teaspoon minced fresh ginger
$\frac{1}{2}$ cup canola oil
2 tablespoons distilled white vinegar
$\frac{1}{4}$ cup maple syrup
4 center-cut pork loin chops

In a food processor, combine the garlic, lemon juice, ginger, oil, vinegar, and maple syrup, and blend until smooth. Place the pork chops in a shallow dish, cover with the sauce, and let stand 15 to 20 minutes.

Prepare a medium-hot fire in a charcoal grill or preheat a gas grill to medium. Grill the pork chops for 5 to 8 minutes. Brush with the sauce and turn. Grill for 5 to 8 minutes on the second side. Transfer to plates and brush with any remaining sauce.

Serves 4

Honey is found in the trees and is gathered amongst briar and bramble bushes.

—Peter Martyr, writing about the New World, 1521

Breads and Other Baked Goods

Blueberry-Maple Muffins

The peak season for blueberries is July and August, but don't let that stop you from making these muffins year-round, since frozen blueberries work well in this recipe. Just be sure you do not let them defrost before adding them to the batter.

1 egg
$\frac{1}{3}$ cup canola oil
$\frac{1}{2}$ cup heavy cream
1 teaspoon maple extract
$\frac{1}{2}$ cup maple syrup
1 $\frac{3}{4}$ cups all-purpose flour
$\frac{1}{2}$ cup granulated sugar
1 teaspoon salt
2 teaspoons baking powder
$\frac{1}{2}$ teaspoon baking soda
2 cups fresh or frozen blueberries
Turbinado sugar, for sprinkling

Preheat the oven to 350 F. Spray 12 muffin cups with vegetable-oil cooking spray.

In a medium bowl, combine the eggs, oil, heavy cream, maple extract, and maple syrup. Whisk to blend well. In a large bowl, combine the flour, granulated sugar, salt, baking powder, and baking soda. Stir to blend. Add the wet ingredients to the dry ingredients and stir just until evenly moistened; the batter will be lumpy. Gently fold in the blueberries. Fill the prepared muffin cups three-fourths full. Sprinkle each muffin with turbinado sugar. Bake for 25 minutes, or until an inserted toothpick comes out clean. Let cool for 5 minutes in the pan, then unmold unto wire racks.

Makes 12 muffins

Maple-Banana Bread with Macadamia Nuts

Macadamia nuts and bananas are perfect partners for maple syrup.

2 cups all-purpose flour

$^1\!/_2$ cup granulated sugar

$^1\!/_4$ cup firmly packed brown sugar

1 $^1\!/_2$ teaspoons baking powder

1 teaspoon baking soda

1 teaspoon salt

1 egg

$^1\!/_2$ cup maple syrup

1 teaspoon maple extract

3 tablespoons unsalted butter, melted

1 $^1\!/_2$ cups mashed ripe bananas

1 cup macadamia nuts, chopped and toasted

Preheat the oven to 350 F. Butter a 9 by 5-inch loaf pan. Sift all the dry ingredients together into a bowl. In another bowl, combine the egg, syrup, extract, butter, and bananas. Whisk to blend. Make a well in the center of the dry ingredients. Add the liquid ingredients all at once. Stir until evenly moistened; the batter will be lumpy. Fold in the nuts. Scrape the batter into the prepared pan. Bake for 1 hour and 30 minutes, or until an inserted tester comes out clean. Let cool in the pan for 5 minutes, then unmold onto a wire rack.

Makes 1 loaf

Maple Granola

You may never use commercial granola again after tasting this recipe.

3 cups old-fashioned rolled oats
$\frac{1}{2}$ cup slivered almonds
$\frac{1}{2}$ cup cashews
$\frac{1}{2}$ cup sesame seeds
$\frac{1}{2}$ cup sunflower seeds
$\frac{1}{2}$ teaspoon salt
$\frac{1}{4}$ cup unsalted butter
$\frac{1}{2}$ cup maple syrup
$\frac{1}{2}$ teaspoon vanilla extract
$\frac{1}{4}$ cup firmly packed brown sugar
1 cup raisins

Preheat the oven to 325 F. In a large bowl, combine the oats, almonds, cashews, sesame seeds, sunflower seeds, and salt.

In a small saucepan, combine the butter, maple syrup, vanilla, and sugar. Cook over medium heat for 5 minutes. Pour over the dry mixture and stir until well blended. Spread the mixture out on a baking sheet in an even layer. Bake, stirring occasionally, for about 20 minutes, or until golden. Remove from the oven and let cool. Stir in the raisins. Store in an airtight container at room temperature for up to 2 weeks.

Makes about 6 cups

Maple–Sweet Potato Biscuits

These biscuits go well at breakfast, lunch, or dinner.

$2\frac{1}{4}$ cups all-purpose flour

1 teaspoon baking powder

$\frac{3}{4}$ teaspoon salt

$\frac{1}{2}$ cup (1 stick) cold unsalted butter, cut into small dice

$\frac{3}{4}$ cup mashed cooked sweet potato

$\frac{1}{3}$ cup maple syrup

$\frac{1}{4}$ cup heavy cream

1 egg, lightly beaten

Preheat the oven to 400 F. Line a baking sheet with parchment paper.

In a food processor, combine the flour, baking powder, and salt. Pulse to combine. Add the butter and pulse until the mixture resembles coarse meal. In a small bowl, combine the sweet potato, maple syrup, and heavy cream. Blend until smooth. Add to the dry mixture and pulse until a soft dough is formed. Turn the dough out onto a lightly floured work surface. Knead the dough 5 times, adding extra flour if necessary. Pat the dough into a 1-inch-thick round. Using a 2-inch cookie cutter, cut out 12 to 16 biscuits and place on the prepared pan. Brush with the beaten egg. Bake for about 20 minutes, or until golden brown. Serve hot.

Makes 12 to 16 biscuits

Maple Shortbread

For a twist, add a tablespoon of grated orange zest.

$^1/_2$ cup (1 stick) unsalted butter, at room temperature
$^1/_4$ cup granulated sugar
$^1/_4$ teaspoon vanilla extract
$^1/_4$ cup maple syrup
1 $^1/_2$ cups all-purpose flour
$^1/_4$ teaspoon salt
1 tablespoon turbinado sugar

Preheat the oven to 325 F. Butter a 9-inch tart pan with a removable bottom.

In a large bowl, using an electric mixer, cream the butter and sugar together for 5 minutes, or until light and fluffy. Beat in the vanilla and syrup. Gradually stir in the flour and salt to make a soft dough. Pat the dough evenly into the prepared pan. Prick the dough with a fork. Sprinkle with turbinado sugar. Bake for 25 to 30 minutes, or until golden. Let cool in the pan for 10 minutes, then unmold and let cool on a wire rack. Cut into 10 wedges.

Makes 10 shortbreads

Maple-Poppy Seed Bread

Make sure the water used to dissolve the yeast is at the proper temperature; too hot will kill the yeast while too cold will cause the dough to take longer to rise.

$^1{}_2$ teaspoon sugar

2 cups warm water (105 F to 115 F)

2 packages active dry yeast

$^1{}_2$ cup maple syrup

3 tablespoons canola oil

2 tablespoons poppy seeds

3 teaspoons salt

5 $^1{}_2$ cups all-purpose flour

1 egg beaten with 1 tablespoon milk

In a large bowl, stir the sugar, water, and yeast together until the yeast is dissolved. Let stand until foamy, about 5 minutes.

Whisk in the maple syrup, oil, poppy seeds, salt, and 2 cups of the flour. Beat until smooth. Using a wooden spoon, stir in the remaining flour $^1{}_2$ cup at a time. Turn the dough out onto a lightly floured surface and knead for 5 minutes, or until smooth and elastic, adding flour, 1 tablespoon at a time, if necessary to keep the dough from sticking. Put the dough in a lightly oiled bowl; turn the dough to coat it with oil. Cover the bowl with plastic wrap and let rise in a warm place until doubled in bulk, about 1 hour. Turn the dough out on a lightly floured board. Divide the dough in half and shape each half into a loaf. Put each loaf in a lightly oiled and floured 9 by 5 by 3-inch loaf pan. Cover with a kitchen towel and let rise in a warm place until the dough reaches the rim of the pans.

Preheat the oven to 375 F. Brush the loaves with the egg mixture. Bake for 30 minutes, or until the loaves are golden brown and sound hollow when tapped.

Makes 2 loaves

Maple Cinnamon Rolls

These gooey rich rolls are a wonderful breakfast treat. For variety, top with chopped pecans.

2 packages active dry yeast

1 tablespoon granulated sugar

$\frac{1}{2}$ cup warm water (105 F to 115 F)

$\frac{1}{2}$ cup (1 stick) unsalted butter, melted

$\frac{1}{2}$ cup heavy cream, warmed

2 eggs, lightly beaten

$\frac{1}{4}$ cup firmly packed brown sugar

$\frac{1}{2}$ teaspoon salt

3 $\frac{1}{2}$ cups all-purpose flour

Topping

$\frac{1}{2}$ cup (1 stick) unsalted butter, room temperature

1 cup firmly packed brown sugar

$\frac{1}{4}$ cup maple syrup

1 tablespoon ground cinnamon

Frosting

1 $\frac{1}{2}$ cups confectioners' sugar

$\frac{1}{3}$ cup maple syrup

2 tablespoons unsalted butter, melted

In a large bowl, stir the yeast and granulated sugar into the warm water until dissolved. Let sit for 10 minutes, or until foamy. Whisk the butter, heavy cream, eggs, brown sugar, and salt into the yeast mixture. Whisk in 2 cups of the flour until smooth. Using a wooden spoon, stir in more flour $\frac{1}{2}$ cup at a time until tacky. Turn the dough out onto a lightly floured work surface. Knead for 5 minutes, or until smooth and elastic. Place in an oiled bowl, turning the dough to coat it. Cover with plastic wrap or a damp cloth and let rise in a warm place for 1 hour, or until doubled in size. Empty the dough out onto a floured surface. Roll out into a large rectangle about $\frac{1}{4}$ inch thick.

To make the topping, combine the butter, brown sugar, and syrup in a bowl. Using an electric mixer, beat until smooth.

Spread the mixture evenly over dough. Sprinkle evenly with the cinnamon. Roll the dough into a log. Cut it into 1-inch-thick slices. Place, cut side down, in a buttered 9 by 13-inch baking dish. Cover with a kitchen towel and let rise in warm place for 30 minutes, or until puffy.

Preheat the oven to 350 F. Bake for 20 minutes.

To make the frosting, combine the confectioners' sugar, syrup, and butter in a bowl. Using an electric mixer, beat until smooth.

Remove the rolls from the oven and let cool completely. Spread the frosting over the top of the rolls. Let stand until set.

Makes 18 rolls

Maple-Sour Cream Coffee Cake

The maple sugar, which is a bit expensive (but worth it), adds great flavor to this coffee cake.

Maple or brown sugar or granulated sugar, for pan

$^1{}_2$ cup (1 stick) unsalted butter, at room temperature

1 cup granulated sugar

3 eggs

$^1{}_2$ teaspoon vanilla extract

$^1{}_2$ cup maple syrup

2 cups sifted all-purpose flour

1 teaspoon baking soda

1 teaspoon baking powder

$^1{}_4$ teaspoon salt

1 cup sour cream

Topping

$^1{}_2$ cup firmly packed light brown sugar

2 tablespoons all-purpose flour

2 tablespoons cold unsalted butter, cut into small pieces

$^1{}_4$ cup chopped almonds

Preheat the oven to 350 F. Butter a 9-inch springform pan and liberally coat with maple sugar. Shake out the excess sugar. Set aside.

In a large bowl, using an electric mixer, cream the butter until smooth. Gradually beat in the 1 cup granulated sugar. Beat in the eggs one at a time and continue to beat until light and fluffy. Beat in the vanilla and maple syrup.

In a medium bowl, combine the flour, baking soda, baking powder, and salt. Stir to blend. Add dry ingredients alternately to the butter with the sour cream. Pour the batter into the prepared pan.

To make the topping, combine the brown sugar, flour, and butter in a medium bowl. Using your fingertips, rub the butter into the mixture until crumbly. Stir in the almonds. Sprinkle the mixture over the cake.

Bake for 30 to 35 minutes, or until the cake is golden and a cake tester inserted in the center comes out clean. Let cool in the pan, then un-mold. Cut into wedges to serve.

Serves 10

Maple Scones

The secret to light flaky scones is to not overwork the dough. A food processor is the best way to incorporate the butter.

    2 cups all-purpose flour

    1 teaspoon salt

    2 tablespoons sugar

    1 teaspoon baking soda

    1 teaspoon baking powder

    $\frac{1}{2}$ cup (1 stick) cold unsalted butter, cut into small dice

    $\frac{1}{4}$ cup maple syrup

    $\frac{1}{2}$ cup plus 1 tablespoon heavy cream

    1 egg

Preheat the oven to 350 F. In a food processor, combine the flour, salt, sugar, baking soda, and baking powder. Pulse to mix. Add the butter and pulse until the mixture resembles coarse cornmeal. Transfer to a large bowl. In another bowl, whisk the maple syrup and the $\frac{1}{2}$ cup cream together. Add to the dry ingredients and stir just until evenly moistened. On a lightly floured work surface, knead the dough gently, about 10 times, or until smooth. Form into a 6-inch disk. Cut the disk into 8 wedges. In a small bowl, beat the egg with the 1 tablespoon cream until blended. Brush the dough with the mixture. Bake for 20 minutes or until golden. Transfer to wire racks to cool slightly. Serve warm.

Makes 8 scones

[Maple syrup is] the most delicious sweet that ever meets the palate.

—Samuel Goodrich,
*Peter Parley's Illustrations
of the Vegetable Kingdom,* 1840

Desserts

Maple-Sweet Potato Pie

Sweet potatoes are incredibly nutritious, containing high amounts of beta-carotene, vitamin C, and vitamin B6. We can feel good about giving this dessert to our children! It is also a nice alternative to pumpkin pie on Thanksgiving.

2 large sweet potatoes
$1/4$ cup unsalted butter, melted
$1/4$ cup firmly packed brown sugar
$1/2$ cup maple syrup
3 large eggs
$3/4$ cup heavy cream
$1/2$ teaspoon vanilla extract
$1/2$ teaspoon maple extract
$1/4$ teaspoon ground cinnamon
$1/4$ teaspoon freshly grated nutmeg
$1/2$ teaspoon salt
1 tablespoon flour
1 unbaked 9-inch pie shell
Whipped cream, for serving

Preheat the oven to 350 F. Bake the sweet potatoes for 1 $1/2$ hours, or until fork tender. Let cool to room temperature.

Preheat oven to 400 F. Scoop the flesh of the potatoes into a small bowl and mash until smooth. Add the butter, brown sugar, and syrup and mix until smooth. In a small bowl, whisk the eggs and heavy cream together. Add to the potato mixture. Whisk in the vanilla, maple extract, cinnamon, nutmeg, salt, and flour until smooth. Pour the mixture into the pie shell. Bake for 45 minutes, or until set. Remove from the oven and let cool completely. Serve with whipped cream.

Serves 8

Maple-Glazed Plantains

This easy but seemingly exotic dessert is excellent served with vanilla ice cream and a delicious sipping rum, such as Barbancourt.

> 3 tablespoons canola oil
> 2 ripe plantains, peeled and cut into $\frac{1}{4}$-inch-thick diagonal slices
> 3 tablespoons maple syrup
> $\frac{1}{4}$ cup pecans, toasted and finely chopped
> Confectioners' sugar, for dusting

Heat the oil in a medium skillet over medium-high heat. Add the plantains and cook for 2 minutes on each side, or until golden brown. Add the syrup, stir to coat, and continue to cook for 3 to 5 minutes, turning once. Transfer to a plate and sprinkle with the pecans. Dust with confectioners' sugar and serve.

Serves 4

Broiled Grapefruit with Maple Syrup

This recipe is great for breakfast or a light dessert. As an alternative, try broiled grapefruit with a dollop of sour cream.

1 ruby red grapefruit, halved
4 teaspoons maple syrup
$\frac{1}{2}$ teaspoon turbinado sugar
1 teaspoon unsalted butter

Preheat the broiler. Using a paring knife, cut between the membranes of the grapefruit. Cut a small piece off the bottom of each grapefruit half so that it sits flat. Drizzle 2 teaspoons syrup on each half, then sprinkle each with $\frac{1}{4}$ teaspoon of sugar and $\frac{1}{2}$ teaspoon of butter. Broil 2 inches from the heat source for 8 minutes, or until golden brown. Serve hot.

Serves 2

Cheddar-Apple-Maple Cobbler

This recipe represents some of the best foods that hail from New England: cheese, syrup, and apples.

$\frac{1}{2}$ cup sugar

$\frac{1}{4}$ cup all-purpose flour

$\frac{1}{4}$ teaspoon ground cinnamon

4 Granny Smith apples, peeled, cored, and coarsely chopped

$\frac{1}{2}$ cup maple syrup

Topping

1 cup all-purpose flour

$\frac{1}{4}$ cup sugar

1 teaspoon baking powder

$\frac{1}{2}$ teaspoon salt

1 cup shredded sharp cheddar cheese

$\frac{1}{3}$ cup unsalted butter, melted

$\frac{1}{4}$ cup heavy cream

Preheat the oven to 400 F. In a small bowl, combine the sugar, flour, and cinnamon. Stir to blend. Put the apples in a large bowl and pour the syrup over. Stir until well coated. Add the sugar mixture and stir to blend. Pour into a 8- or 9-inch square baking dish and set aside.

To make the topping, combine the flour, sugar, baking powder, and salt and mix well. Add the cheddar cheese and mix well. Add the butter and cream, mixing until well blended. Spoon over the apple mixture and bake for 30 minutes, or until golden brown. Serve immediately.

Serves 6

Pear-Maple Upside-Down Cake

While pineapple is the traditional fruit used in this recipe, pears are a wonderful substitute. The juice from the pears, sugar, and syrup caramelize to make a beautiful glaze.

$\frac{1}{2}$ cup (1 stick) unsalted butter

$\frac{1}{4}$ cup firmly packed brown sugar

$\frac{1}{4}$ cup maple syrup

2 firm but ripe Bosc pears, peeled, cored, and sliced thin

Batter

1 $\frac{1}{2}$ cups all-purpose flour

1 teaspoon baking powder

$\frac{1}{2}$ teaspoon salt

$\frac{1}{2}$ teaspoon ground cinnamon

$\frac{1}{2}$ cup (1 stick) unsalted butter, at room temperature

$\frac{3}{4}$ cup granulated sugar

1 teaspoon vanilla extract

2 eggs

1 cup milk

Preheat the oven to 350 F. In a medium skillet, combine the butter, brown sugar, and maple syrup. Cook over medium heat, stirring constantly, until thickened, about 5 minutes. Arrange the pears in a spiral pattern in a 9-inch round cake pan and pour the syrup over the pears.

To make the batter, combine the flour, baking powder, salt, and cinnamon in a medium bowl. In a large bowl, using an electric mixer, beat the butter and sugar together until light and fluffy. Beat in the vanilla, then the eggs, one at a time. Beat in the milk, then gradually beat in the dry ingredients until smooth.

Spoon the batter over the topping. Bake for 40 minutes, or until an inserted toothpick comes out clean. Transfer the pan to a wire rack to cool. Run a knife around the edges of the pan and invert onto a serving platter.

Makes one 9-inch cake

Lemon Pound Cake with Maple Glaze

In England in the eighteenth century, pound cake was made with one pound (Imperial measurement) each of flour, butter, eggs, and sugar. The result was, and is, a rich, dense, moist cake.

> 1 $\frac{3}{4}$ cups all-purpose flour
>
> 1 $\frac{1}{2}$ teaspoons baking powder
>
> $\frac{1}{2}$ teaspoon salt
>
> 1 cup (2 sticks) unsalted butter, at room temperature
>
> 1 $\frac{1}{2}$ cups sugar
>
> 4 eggs
>
> 1 teaspoon vanilla extract
>
> $\frac{1}{4}$ cup heavy cream
>
> $\frac{1}{4}$ cup freshly squeezed lemon juice

Glaze

> 2 tablespoons unsalted butter
>
> $\frac{1}{4}$ cup maple syrup
>
> $\frac{3}{4}$ cup confectioners' sugar, sifted

Preheat the oven to 350 F. Spray a 9 by 5 by 3-inch loaf pan with vegetable-oil cooking spray.

In a medium bowl, combine the flour, baking powder, and salt.

In a large bowl, using an electric mixer, cream the butter and sugar together until light and fluffy. Beat in the eggs one at a time. Add the vanilla. Beat in half of the dry ingredients, then the heavy cream and lemon juice. Beat in the remaining dry ingredients just until smooth. Pour into the prepared pan and bake for 60 to 75 minutes, or until an inserted tester comes out clean.

Meanwhile, make the glaze: In a small saucepan, melt the butter. Add maple syrup and cook over medium-low heat for 3 minutes. Add the sugar and whisk until smooth. Remove from the heat. Let cool for 10 minutes. Pour over the cake and let stand until the glaze sets.

Makes 1 loaf cake

Apple Fritters with Maple Cream Sauce

These dessert fritters can just as easily be made with bananas or strawberries.

   1 cup sifted all-purpose flour
   2 tablespoons sugar
   1 teaspoon baking powder
   $\frac{1}{2}$ teaspoon salt
   $\frac{1}{2}$ teaspoon ground cinnamon
   1 egg
   $\frac{1}{2}$ cup milk
   $\frac{1}{2}$ cup maple syrup
   1 cup heavy cream
   $\frac{1}{3}$ cup canola oil
   1 Granny Smith apple, peeled, cored, and cut into $\frac{1}{4}$-inch-
      thick slices
   Confectioners' sugar, for dusting

Sift the flour, sugar, baking powder, salt, and cinnamon together into a medium bowl. In a small bowl, whisk the egg and milk together until blended. Whisk the wet ingredients into the flour mixture until smooth. Let rest in the refrigerator for 30 minutes.

In a small saucepan, combine the maple syrup and heavy cream. Bring to a simmer over medium heat and cook for 5 minutes, or until thickened slightly. Remove from the heat and set aside.

In a medium skillet, heat the oil over medium-high heat until it shimmers. Dip the apple slices in the batter. Drop the slices one at a time into the oil and fry until golden brown, about 2 minutes per side. Transfer to paper towels to drain. Dust with confectioners' sugar and serve immediately with maple cream as a dipping sauce.

Serves 4

Strawberry-Stuffed Crêpes with Mascarpone and Orange-Maple Syrup

Crêpes can be made ahead and frozen between sheets of waxed paper.

Crêpe Batter

> 1 cup all-purpose flour
>
> 1 egg
>
> 1 egg yolk
>
> 1 tablespoon unsalted butter, melted
>
> $\frac{1}{2}$ teaspoon salt
>
> 2 teaspoons sugar
>
> 1 $\frac{1}{4}$ cups milk

Filling

> 2 cups fresh strawberries, hulled and sliced
>
> $\frac{1}{4}$ cup strawberry jam
>
> 4 tablespoons sugar
>
> $\frac{1}{2}$ cup mascarpone cheese, at room temperature

Syrup

> $\frac{1}{2}$ cup maple syrup
>
> 2 tablespoons freshly squeezed orange juice
>
> Canola oil, for cooking crêpes

To make the batter, combine the flour, egg, egg yolk, butter, salt, sugar, and milk in a medium bowl. Whisk well to blend and set aside.

To make the filling, combine the strawberries, jam, and 2 tablespoons of the sugar in a small saucepan. Cook, stirring occasionally, over medium heat for 5 minutes, or until warm. In a small bowl, combine the mascarpone cheese and the remaining 2 tablespoons sugar. Blend well and set aside.

To make the syrup, combine the maple syrup and orange juice in a small saucepan. Warm over low heat for 5 minutes, or until slightly thickened.

Lightly oil a 12-inch nonstick crêpe pan or skillet. Heat the pan over medium-high heat. Pour a scant $\frac{1}{4}$ cup batter into the pan and quickly swirl to coat the pan. Cook for 1 minute, or until golden. Turn and cook on the other side for 1 minute more, or until the bottom appears lightly browned and the crêpe slides easily in the pan. Repeat to cook the remaining batter. You should have 8 crêpes.

To assemble, spread 1 tablespoon of the mascarpone mixture over a crêpe. Using a slotted spoon, scoop $\frac{1}{4}$ cup strawberries and place in a line down the center of the crêpe. Roll up the crêpe. Repeat with remaining crêpes. Serve 2 crêpes per person with a little orange-maple syrup drizzled over.

Serves 4

Peanut Butter–Maple Cookies

Use natural peanut butter (which has no added sugar) for these cookies if you can.

- $\frac{1}{2}$ cup (1 stick) unsalted butter, at room temperature
- 1 cup smooth or chunky natural peanut butter
- $\frac{1}{2}$ cup firmly packed brown sugar
- $\frac{1}{4}$ cup granulated sugar
- $\frac{1}{2}$ cup maple syrup
- 1 egg
- $\frac{1}{2}$ teaspoon vanilla extract
- 1 $\frac{1}{2}$ cups all-purpose flour
- 1 teaspoon baking soda
- $\frac{1}{4}$ teaspoon salt

Preheat the oven to 350 F. In a medium bowl, using an electric mixer, cream the butter, peanut butter, and sugars together until light and fluffy. Beat in the maple syrup, egg, and vanilla until smooth. In a large bowl, combine the flour, baking soda, and salt. Stir to blend. Add the wet ingredients and mix just until combined. Using a tablespoon, scoop out the dough and form into balls. Place 2 inches apart on an ungreased baking sheet. Flatten in a crisscross pattern with a fork. Bake for 15 minutes, or until lightly browned. Transfer to a wire rack to cool.

Makes 2 $\frac{1}{2}$ dozen cookies

Maple-Pecan Pie

After arriving in New Orleans in the late 1600s, the French were introduced to pecans by Native Americans, and shortly thereafter the first pecan pie was made. It's delicious alone, or served with vanilla ice cream.

   3 eggs
   1 cup firmly packed brown sugar
   $\frac{1}{4}$ cup granulated sugar
   $\frac{1}{2}$ teaspoon salt
   2 tablespoons all-purpose flour
   1 cup maple syrup
   3 tablespoons unsalted butter, melted
   1 $\frac{1}{2}$ cups pecans
   1 unbaked 9-inch pie shell

Preheat the oven to 400 F. In a medium bowl, combine the eggs, sugars, salt, flour, syrup and butter. Whisk until well blended. Stir in the pecans. Pour into the pie shell and bake for 45 minutes, or until set.

Makes 1 pie

Nana's Maple Nut Fudge

This is from my good friend's grandmother Amanda Davison Aplin of Craftsbury Common, Vermont.

2 tablespoons unsalted butter

1 cup sugar

2 cups maple syrup

$\frac{2}{3}$ cup heavy cream

$\frac{1}{4}$ teaspoon salt

1 cup chopped walnuts

In a deep, heavy pot, melt the butter over medium heat. Add the sugar, syrup, heavy cream, and salt. Stir until the sugar is dissolved. Bring to a boil and cook without stirring to 240 F. (A drop of the mixture will form a firm ball in glass of ice water.) This happens quickly, so keep watch!

Remove from the heat and stir almost constantly for about 10 minutes, or until almost fully thickened. Stir in the chopped nuts and blend evenly throughout the fudge. Turn immediately into a buttered 8- or 9-inch square pan.

Let cool thoroughly, score into 1-inch pieces, and store in an airtight container.

Makes 64 pieces

About the Author

Jennifer Trainer Thompson is an accomplished cook,
a James Beard Award nominee, and author or coauthor of seven cookbooks
and two nonfiction books. Her articles have appeared in the
New York Times, Travel & Leisure, Diversion, Omni, and Harvard.
Thompson is the owner and chef of the Jump Up & Kiss Me brand of food products
and has her own brand of maple syrup, Upside Down Maple Syrup.
Thompson lives with her family in rural Massachusetts.